QATAR

Text & Photos

CHRISTINE OSBORNE

First published in 2018.

osbchristine@gmail.com
www.paperhorsedesign.com.au

Author   Christine Osborne
Title: Old Gulf Coast Days: Qatar
ISBN: 9780992324049 (paperback)
Subjects: Qatar
                Pictorial works
                Local history
              Traditional life
              Bedouin-Crafts
              Archaeology
              Architecture
              Environment
              Nature and Wildlife
              Agriculture-Date Farming

Cover photo: Fishing boats in al-Ruwais, Christine Osborne
Page 36: Falcon market in Doha, Jill Brown.

A catalogue reference for this book is available
from The National Library of Australia

My involvement with Qatar began in 1975 when I visited the tiny Gulf state to research my book *The Gulf States and Oman*. At that time the capital Doha was still a sleepy backwater with a single first class hotel, one bank and no tourist office.

Qatar was a slow starter in development compared with its Arab neighbours. While the country was accruing revenues from prodigious oil and gas deposits, its ruler was reluctant to accelerate change. There was also the problem among the Qatari elite in deciding which families owned the valuable real estate on West Bay. But this said, change came—albeit slowly.

Lacking any natural water resources, Qatar made an early investment in a desalination plant to provide potable water for a thirsty population. In 1974, the first fodder crop— mainly lucerne irrigated by bore-water — was sown near the Saudi border. 350 cows were imported from Holland to launch a dairy industry and 15,000 chickens from Lebanon to start a poultry industry. And a National Museum, housed in a former palace, opened its doors. Among the first visitors was HM Queen Elizabeth on her historic tour of the Arabian peninsula in 1979.

Real development in Qatar began in earnest only when HH Sheikh Hamad bin Khalifa al-Thani came to power in 1995. A thoroughly modern ruler, under his auspices a sky-high city rose from the desert in less than a decade. Launched by emiri decree in 1996, al Jazeera satellite channel began broadcasting to a worldwide audience and in 1997, Qatar Airways made its inaugural flight to London.

This book, however, is not an appraisal of 21st century Qatar. It is a look back, via a unique set of photographs, at 'Old Gulf Coast' days of the 1970s.

CHRISTINE OSBORNE

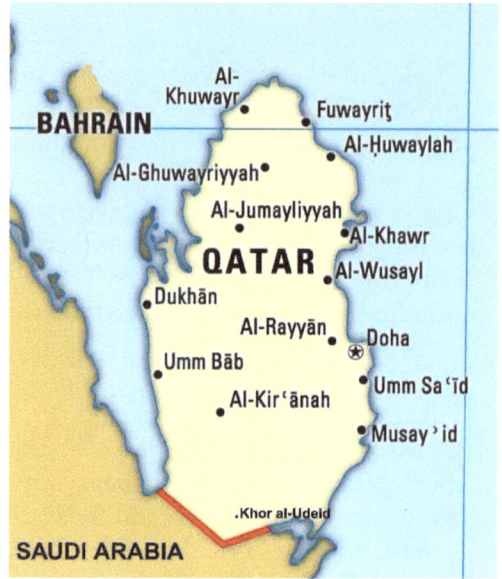

Qatar is an independent Arab state projecting into the Gulf from mainland Saudi Arabia. An hereditary monarchy, it has been ruled by the al-Thani family of sheikhs since the 19th century. The country became a British Protectorate in 1916, but when the Maritime Treaty of Peace in Perpetuity was annulled in 1970, it opted for independence from the other Trucial States. Qatar was one of the world's poorest nations until the discovery of oil in 1939. Native Qataris, who comprise just 12% of the majority migrant population, today enjoy a high standard of living. Most people live in the capital Doha, a former pearling port on the central east coast.

In the early 1970s, Qatar flared about 80% of the 16.8 km³ of natural gas produced daily in association with crude oil liftings in the major onshore field at Dukhan.

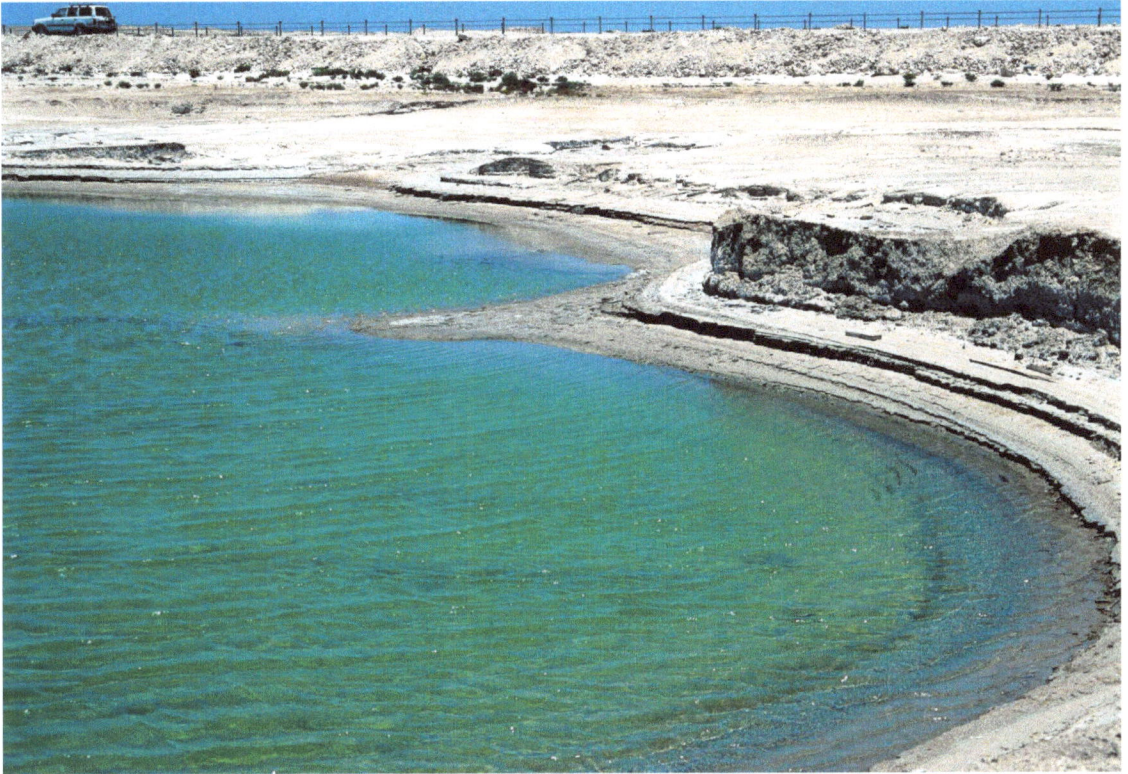

The peninsula of Qatar extends north into the Gulf for 160 km varying in width between 55-90 km. The landscape is a low-lying pebble conglomerate punctuated by limestone outcrops becoming true desert around the saltwater inlet of Khor al-Udeid on the Saudi border. Intense heat and humidity characterise the climate and while rainfall is minimal, it sustains arid-zone shrubs and perennial grasses. Qatar has no natural freshwater and a limited amount of underground water is too salty to use in agriculture making it dependent on desalination plants. Salt pans (above) are a feature of the east coastline. The Desert Hyacinth (left) is actually a parasitic herb common in coastal areas.

The Arabian oryx – *Oryx leucoryx* – is the largest land mammal native to Qatar. An elegant cream animal with scimitar-like horns and a distinctive shoulder hump, it was able to thrive in the harsh environment, often walking 70km a night in search of sparse grasses; like the camel, needing little water. Hunting parties from Saudi Arabia brought the oryx to the brink of extinction in the early 1970s, but from two animals, a member of the al-Thani ruling family built up a private herd. Once endangered, the noble oryx has been downgraded to vulnerable by the ICUN, thanks to the ancestors of these captive animals, pictured in 1976. The much smaller Rheem or Desert Gazelle, also once hunted ruthlessly in the Arabian peninsula, also now enjoys protection.

At first sight, the desert appears devoid of wildlife, but footprints in the sand reveal the presence of small nocturnal creatures that hide away from searing daytime temperatures. These vertical tracks were likely made by a desert jerboa. Perhaps a pair of these tiny mammals were hunting moths and other insects. Clearly night witnessed a scuffle - possibly a Horned Viper chasing a lizard of which Qatar records some 21 species, notably of the gecko family. Dew collecting on plants sustains larger animals such as Ruepell's Fox and the Arabian Sand Cat. Hedgehogs are found and much rarer Honey Badgers in the south-west of the peninsula. 215 species of birds have been identified in Qatar, both local and migratory species.

In former times domestic livestock was limited to camels and goats able to survive in the arid environment. The Bedouin kept camels not only for milk, but for a myriad other uses. Urine from a she-camel acted as a purgative and antiseptic. Dried camel dung was used as fuel for desert camp-fires. And nothing was wasted when an animal was slaughtered for a tribal feast. The hide was woven into belts and saddle bags, the hair for weaving rugs. Goats served as milk and meat. Goat skin was fashioned into buckets for carrying water and bags for making buttermilk. Opposite, Indian migrant workers oversee a herd in the hinterland.

Dates are historically an important crop in Qatar. Until the 1970s, due to a lack of water and poor quality soil, date palms were the only form of cultivation. Improved farming methods now see date production account for 7.2% of the total agricultural output. Counting more than 500,000 palm trees, Qatar is self sufficient in some 20 varieties of dates, including the most popular types such as *ajwa, medjool and khenazi*. The exception is the holy month of Ramadan when demand is greater since dates are traditionally eaten first when Muslims break their daily fast at dusk.

Pearling was the main source of income for the majority of Qatar's inhabitants until the first oil exports in the late forties. Pearl harvesting was traditionally divided into three periods: *Hansiyah* commencing mid-April and lasting 40 days, *Ghaus al Kebir*, the primary diving season, May to September and *Ruddah* Sept-October. The boats or *sambuqs* were able to remain out for long periods due to fresh-water springs bubbling in the sea-bed which, by holding a goatskin bag over the source, divers could replenish their supply. The pearls were mainly sent to markets in Bombay for classification. Following pages show an aerial view of Khor al-Udeid, the great inland sea, 78 kilometres south-east of Doha.

165 species of fish have been recorded in the Gulf off Qatar which has some 560 km of coastline. Common varieties are bream, snapper, grouper, barracuda, kingfish and mackerel. The most popular eating fish is the rock cod or *hamour* in Arabic. Fishing is traditionally carried out using nets, lines and large hand woven wire traps known as *gandours*. The image opposite shows a tidal fish trap constructed of lumps of coral near the north east town of al-Khawr. When the sea recedes, the trapped fish are captured in a hand net. Parrot fish, above, have a beak-like mouth which can rasp algae off the coral.

Stone Age tools unearthed in Qatar indicate human habitation from at least 5 BCE. The first known map referenced the peninsula as *Catara*. Among finds were Kassite potsherds and millions of crushed molluscs, evidence of an early shellfish dye industry. Chinese porcelain and East African coins indicate far flung trade links, while records from the Umayyad period describe a famous horse and camel breeding centre. Dated to the 8th century, pearling continued unbroken until the collapse of the entire Gulf pearl industry in the 1930s. The north coast town of al-Zubarah flourished as a pearling and trading centre until the early 1900s before being destroyed in 1811 and abandoned in the early 1900s. Archaeological remains of houses, aqueducts and public buildings in the area suggest local prosperity. al-Zubarah Fort, above, was built in 1938. Opposite, top left, a well head constructed from coral stone. The following pages depict an aerial view of coastal villages south of Doha in 1976.

The 1970s saw a considerable number of traditional Qatari buildings being refurbished or more often than not, being demolished and rebuilt. The owner of this once grand old mansion is rendering its crumbling coral stone walls with cement. Old hand carved doors were once a feature on local houses like the one in the photo, its teak bleached by salt laden winds. When modern steel doors became the vogue, fine old doors like the entrance to this mosque in al-Wakrah, 20 km south of Doha, were consigned to the rubbish heap.

The ruins of an Islamic dwelling, carbon-dated to the 7th century, indicate the town of al-Wakrah, south of Doha, has been settled since this time. This once majestic old mansion with fine plaster patterns was being demolished in 1975. *Naqsh* was a popular early decoration, usually found in the reception room and in the *harem* of such houses owned by a wealthy merchant. In early times the patterns, drawn quickly in the drying plaster, were likely done by former pearl divers or fishermen no longer able to perform heavy work. Later the craft became more sophisticated with master masons carrying on the tradition, but still adhering to the geometric patterns characteristic of Islamic art.

Lorimer's *Gazeteer of the Persian Gulf*, published in 1905, describes al-Ruwais as a coastal village at the tip of the Qatar peninsula inhabited by about 70 families who own 18 pearl boats, 2 other sea-going vessels and 10 fishing boats which find safe anchorage inside a reef. Like other coastal buildings, the houses were constructed from what was known as *juss bahar* or beach plaster made by mixing coral stone and shells which were dried and then set in gypsum mortar. The material is evident in this crumbling house in al-Ruwais.

Weaving was a popular pastime for Bedouin women spending most of the day in their tent. A tent was traditionally woven from a mixture of goat hair and wool with strips of linen added for extra strength. A tent was ideally suited to a desert environment being easy to erect and dismantle and load onto a camel for transportation to a new campsite. These Bedouin wives were photographed in 1975. Until oil revenues became available, many Bedouin lived a peripatetic existence linked to locating pasture for their animals.

Hand woven items made by Bedouin women include mats, cushion covers, camel saddle blankets and the all important curtain, or *sahah*, which divides the tent into two sections. The women's domain for cooking and sleeping, the other for eating and entertaining by the men. The choice of flamboyant colors used in the textiles was likely a reaction to living in the generally neutral-toned environment.

While gold is now the preference, in former times Gulf Bedouin wore silver jewellery received as a wedding present. As well as being appreciated for its ornamental attraction, jewellery was valued as a readily available bank should cash be needed. Wealthier women wore heavier more dramatic pieces like the anklet and earring pictured. Poorer brides were given cheaper items such as the pendant (top) but which was no less important such as this piece with a case containing a favourite verse *sura* from the Qur'an.

Souq Waqif, Doha's central market, was likely founded more than a century ago. Its small shops sold household items and traditional clothing, perfumes, henna and other beauty products, fruit and vegetables, spices and fresh fish. There was a separate section for the Bedouin to buy and sell hunting falcons while outside, on a patch of sand, professional scribes assisted migrants with work applications. The woman wears the mask *burqa* and cloak, *abaya,* fashion of Muslim women in the Arab States of the Gulf.

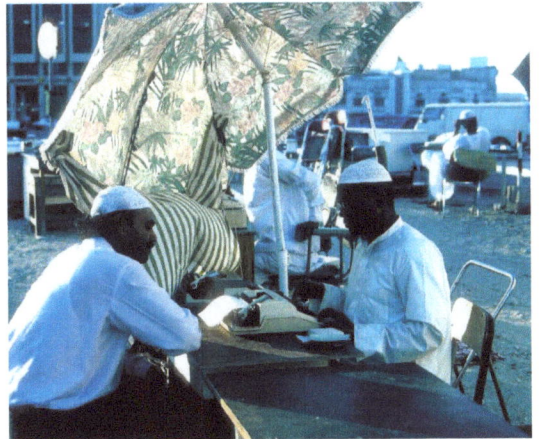

Oil was discovered at Dukhan on the west coast, 80 km from Doha. Top right depicts the original well head spudded in 1938. Exports, delayed by the start of the Second World War, began in the late 1940s. By the mid-1970s, Dukhan was pumping peak levels of 500,000 barrels a day. In 1960, Qatar's first off-shore oil field was located. Subsequent discoveries in the Gulf, 180 km north of Doha, include the world's third largest natural gas reserves and an estimated 25 billion barrels of oil. Umm Said oil refinery was built in 1953.

Old Gulf coast style architecture on a shop-house in Doha. Opposite page, the Qatar National Bank, the first locally owned financial institution established in 1965.

البشت
القطري ▶

قطر
خصوصي
**QATAR
PRIVATE**

١٢٩٧٨
12978

Central Doha 1970s

West Bay tea-house

First desalination plant

Exercising race camels

Irrigated lucerne field

Doha dhow harbour

Original dairy herd

Locally produced milk

National Museum 1975

Monuments in Doha reflect it's not so distant past. Following pages depict a view across West Bay from the city centre with the new Sheraton Hotel, 1979.

www.ingramcontent.com/pod-product-compliance
Lightning Source LLC
Chambersburg PA
CBHW061152030426
42336CB00002B/24